Animals That Live on the Farm

Horses

By JoAnn Early Macken

Reading Consultant: Jeanne Clidas, Ph.D.
Director, Roberts Wesleyan College Literacy Clinic

WEEKLY READER®
PUBLISHING

Please visit our web site at **www.garethstevens.com**.
For a free catalog describing our list of high-quality books,
call 1-877-542-2595 (USA) or 1-800-387-3178 (Canada).
Our fax: 1-877-542-2596

Library of Congress Cataloging-in-Publication Data

Macken, JoAnn Early, 1953–
      Horses / by JoAnn Early Macken.
         p. cm. — (Animals that live on the farm)
      Includes bibliographical references and index.
      ISBN-10: 1-4339-2398-X   ISBN-13: 978-1-4339-2398-2 (lib. bdg.)
      ISBN-10: 1-4339-2467-6   ISBN-13: 978-1-4339-2467-5 (soft cover)
      1. Horses—Juvenile literature. I. Title.
SF302.M248   2010
636.1—dc22   2009004177

This edition first published in 2010 by
Weekly Reader® Books
An Imprint of Gareth Stevens Publishing
1 Reader's Digest Road
Pleasantville, NY 10570-7000 USA

Copyright © 2010 by Gareth Stevens, Inc.

Executive Managing Editor: Lisa M. Herrington
Senior Editor: Barbara Bakowski
Project Management: Spooky Cheetah Press
Cover Designers: Jennifer Ryder-Talbot and Studio Montage
Production: Studio Montage
Library Consultant: Carl Harvey, Library Media Specialist, Noblesville, Indiana

Photo credits: Cover, pp. 1, 5, 7, 9, 21 Shutterstock; p. 11 © Alan and Sandy Carey; pp. 13, 15, 17 © Sharon Eide and Elizabeth Flynn/SandEphoto.com; p. 19 © Gregg Andersen

Printed in China

2 3 4 5 6 7 8 9 14 13 12 11 10 09

Table of Contents

Boldface words appear in the glossary.

Growing Up

A baby horse is called a **foal**. A foal can stand soon after it is born.

foal

A foal drinks milk from its mother. A grown female horse is called a **mare**. In a few weeks, the foal is ready to eat grass.

mare

On a farm, horses also eat hay, oats, and grain. They need fresh water every day.

When a horse is one year old, it is called a **yearling**. A yearling is old enough to learn to carry a rider.

yearling

Horses walk and **trot**. They also **gallop** fast! Horses can sleep standing up.

Super Senses

A horse's eyes are on the sides of its head. The horse can see straight ahead and to the sides. Horses can even see what is behind them!

eyes

Horses hear very well.
They can turn their ears
toward sounds.

ears

Many Types of Horses

Some horses, called **ponies**, are very small. Other horses are very big. A large horse can weigh as much as a small car!

pony

Some people ride horses for fun. Other people use horses for work. Some farmers use horses to carry loads or pull wagons.

Fast Facts

Height	up to about 7 feet (2 meters) at the shoulder
Length	up to about 7 feet (2 meters) nose to tail
Weight	up to about 3,000 pounds (1,361 kilograms)
Diet	grass, oats, grain, and hay
Average life span	up to 30 years

Glossary

foal: a baby horse

gallop: run

mare: a grown female horse

ponies: small horses

trot: move at a pace between walking and running

yearling: a horse that is one year old

For More Information

Books

Sesame Subjects: My First Book About Horses and Ponies.
Kama Einhorn (Random House, 2008)

What Happens at a Horse Farm?
Where People Work (series). Amy Hutchings
(Gareth Stevens, 2009)

Web Sites

Horses at Enchanted Learning
www.enchantedlearning.com/themes/horse.shtml
Print out a diagram that you can color.

The Ultimate Horse Site
www.ultimatehorsesite.com
Play games and listen to real horse sounds.

Index

About the Author

JoAnn Early Macken is the author of two rhyming picture books, *Sing-Along Song* and *Cats on Judy*, and more than 80 nonfiction books for children. Her poems have appeared in several children's magazines. She lives in Wisconsin with her husband and their two sons.